TINY
TREASURES

MARY KOSKI

ISLAND HERITAGE™
PUBLISHING

For my grandchildren:
Megan,
Kristoffer,
Anastasia,
Allison,
Kaitrin, and Brendan

And
all the beautiful little keiki
I so love to paint.

Introduction

This mini book presents Hawai'i's Tiny Treasures—its keiki (children)—as only Mary Koski can present them. Found within these pages are delightful paintings and precious poems that Mary Koski has created during many years of living in the Islands . . . and enjoying its Tiny Treasures.

A Little Water Music

The little creatures of the sea
Leave their watery world so dim
To hear the pretty melody
The child is playing just for them.
Little wiggly, squishy things
Her audience will be—
And when her song is finished,
They'll return into the sea.

Carissa

Sweet little girl
From far away—
You've crept into
Our hearts to stay.

Sunday's Child

Sunday's child is nice and neat—
Her hat on straight, shoes on her feet.
So soon that pristine look she'll lose—
Where is her hat?
Where are her shoes?
But, it's nice to see her at her peak—
Even if it's just once a week!

Golden Children

Golden Children of the sun—
Dashing, flashing,
Having fun.
Laughing, playing
Here and there.
Dancing feet and
Flying hair.

End of an Era

Where have you gone, Kaiulani?
Your peacocks are crying for you
   on the lawn.
Where have you gone, Kaiulani?
Where have you gone?

On Stage

Here I am, up on the stage—
And I am scared to death!
My little heart is pounding—
I can hardly get my breath!

But Mom and Dad and Bro and Sis
Are there with all the rest . . .
The cousins, aunts and uncles—
So, I have to do my best.

Coconut Boy

I like to help my Grandpa—
I've helped him all my life,
But I'd do better with this coconut
If he'd let me use a knife.

Secret Treasures

The sea is full of treasures
But they're guarded jealously
By water sprites and mermaids
For they are their property.
The ocean's full of secrets
Only seen by those
Who live beneath the water
And know things that no child knows.

The Case for Babies

Children are nice
  But babies are nicer!
They don't
  completely wreck
  the room,
  spill (or drink)
  your best perfume,
  track in dirt,
  or stray dogs and cats,
  make mud pies
  in visitors' hats,
  tear their clothes,
  lose their shoes,
  skin their noses,
  spread the news,

bring home chicken pox,
colds and flus,
keep the neighbors
on needles and pins,
give black eyes
to their best friends,
wander away,
scare you
out of your wits,
trade their only
sweater that fits
for some well-chewed gum
and a worn-out ball.
They don't drive you crazy
Or right up the wall...

YET

23

Balloons

Brother and me have
Lots of balloons of red and pink
    and blue.
I think there's nothing prettier
Than a big balloon, don't you?

May Day

She's just been chosen
   May Day Queen!
Her dress is new, her face is clean.
She must sit upon that chair,
And everyone she knows will stare.
All she is or does is seen.
She wishes someone else was queen!

The Hikers

In these misty, magic mountains
My dog and I can roam,
And when we're tired and hungry
Why, then we just go home.

Waimea Girl

Young girl of the highlands,
Child of cool breezes and of
*   dewy meadows—*
I hope you realize what you possess.

Blue Ginger

Koi fish are always hungry
For something good to eat.
Isn't it a wonder they don't
Nibble at her feet!

Koi

Sing a song of fishes
Swimming in a pool—
Here comes a golden one
Shining like a jewel.

First Son

Happy, laughing
Little boy.
Daddy's pride
And Mama's joy.
Grandpa's buddy,
Grandma's dove—
Darling child
Just made to love!

Keiki Hula

Sassy little hula girl,
Give your ti leaf skirt a whirl.
Talking hands and dancing feet
Harking to the ipu beat.

Paniolo Boy

Daddy is a cowboy
And I will be one, too.
When I get my pony,
Here's what I will do.

At the rodeo, I'll rope the calves
And everyone will clap.
I ride the race and win the cup—
And then I'll take my nap.

Kristoffer at Two

Bright blue eyes, tousled hair,
Little lad without a care.
Chubby legs, dimpled arms.
Full of beans and full of charms.
Keeps his Grandpa on his toes,
And his Grandma—
Goodness knows!

Never still
Never quiet,
Always there to start a riot.
Fingers in the cookie jar,
Eyes upon a far-off star.
Busy, busy
Never done—
Everything is at a run.
This special age is so soon past,
Darling, don't grow up too fast!

43

Waiting in the Wings

She knows she has
A lot to learn,
But someday it will
Be her turn.
Until that day
The future brings,
She's happy waiting
In the wings.

Dancing in the Sunlight

The air is warm and smells
   of flowers—
It is so clear and fresh, it feels almost
   like water on my skin.
When the ti leaf skirts swirl,
The scent is so sweet that I can't keep
   from breaking into a smile!

White Ginger

Gentle maiden, will you wear
Some ginger flowers in your hair?
Their innocence and budding grace
Are all reflected in your face.

Aunty Anna's Pool

Down to Aunty Anna's pool
Where the water's deep and cool
And the water lilies grow—
That is where I long to go.
There I played when just a child
When skies were always blue
   and mild,
And my life seemed a simple chain
Of carefree days with little rain.

Kolohe

What can we think of
That we haven't done?
Something exciting
That has to be fun!
Grandma's knitting got snarled
But you kittens did that,
And I hid Mama's chocolate
So she wouldn't get fat.

I've drawn on the wall
A most beautiful view—
Put your paws in the ink
And you can paint, too.
If we cut the flowers,
We could plant a whole row—
Oh! I hear Mama coming!
Come on, guys, **let's go!**

Two Roses

Lokilani, Maui's rose—
Sweet and pink as baby's toes.
Blooming beneath tropic skies,
Bright and clear as baby's eyes.
Silken petals, blushing tips,
Rosy red as baby's lips.
Shall we call her by your name?
Baby and Rose—so much the same.

The Question of Shell Ginger

How did God convince
All those pretty shells to hang clustered
   on one stem?
And what miracle
Changes them into
Bright yellow flowers?
Is it truly a miracle or merely magic?
Don't you wish you knew?

Sweet Dreams

"Sleep, little lady,"
The breezes sigh,
"And the bees will hum you a lullaby.
As your book falls forgotten
To the floor
Fairies will steal in
Through the door—
Then each will take you
By the hand
And lead you into fairyland."

'Ōhelo Berries

The breeze is cool,
The sun is hot.
Your basket's full—
But mine is not.
Beside the berry bush you squat
And pick the berries as you ought.
But I, upon my back have lain
And thought how nice there is no rain
How sweet the bird song, bright
   and clear—
How dear the earth this time of year.

Twin Math

4 little eyes

4 little ears

They add up to 2 little dears

4 little hands

4 little feet

All add up to 2 things sweet

2 pert noses

2 big grins

They add up to 1 set of twins!

Sunday School

Each week I go to Sunday School
And there I learn the Golden Rule.
I learn to tell the rights from wrongs—
But most of all, I like the songs!

Tūtū's Chair

In Tūtū's chair,
I wile away
The happy hours,
Day by day.

Island Sisters

Little sisters
Dressed in white—
Don't they make
A pretty sight?
Decked with flowers
In their hair—
Natural jewels
For them to wear,
Sharing dreams
That both have made
While sitting
In the dappled shade.

Leilani's Castle

I've built a castle in the sand—
It's very fine and strong.
A flag flies from its very top,
But it won't last for long.
I fear the tide is coming in,
My castle to surround...
It's good that no one lives there
For they would soon be drowned!

Waimea Greens

Pretty little Anna lives
Amid green velvet hills.
Where cattle roam
And horses graze,
She spends her happy childhood days.
The gentle rain falls sweetly
Upon the emerald fields—
Where breezes blow
And gingers grow,
Riches gleam in each rainbow.

Aloha Boy

His eyes look out across the sea—
His future's still a mystery.
His book of life—few pages turned,
And up to now—few lessons learned.
Someday he'll travel far away . . .
But then he will come home to stay.

Malia's Quilt

This quilt is mine and don't you see,
My *tūtū* sewed it just for me.
And when it's time to go to bed,
I'll pull my quilt above my head,
And pat it down and hold it tight—
My quilt and I will say, "Good night."

Garden Fairies

There are fairies in the garden.
I know—for I've seen them there.
There are little boys with pointy ears.
And girls with long, bright hair.

Their wings are full of rainbows
And their colors shift and change.
But they're also like the butterflies—
Most wonderful and strange.

They are very shy and private
And they don't like to be seen,
But I'd rather glimpse a fairy
Than meet a reigning Queen!

About the Author/Artist

Mary Koski's paintings create light and life
that seem to glow from within the art itself.
A resident of Waimea on the Big Island of
Hawai'i, Koski has found exciting inspira-
tion in the ancient forms of hula and the
rich beauty of Hawaiian faces, especially
those of Island children.